Bertram Brooker

1888–1955

Bertram Brooker lecturing on abstract
art at the Art Gallery of Toronto, *c*. 1949.

Bertram Brooker

Dennis Reid

Series edited by Dennis Reid
Curator of Post-Confederation Art
National Gallery of Canada

CANADIAN ARTISTS SERIES

1

NATIONAL GALLERY OF CANADA
NATIONAL MUSEUMS OF CANADA
OTTAWA

1979

© National Gallery of Canada
for
the Corporation of the National Museums of Canada
Ottawa, 1973
Second printing with augmented illustration, 1979.

ISBN 0-88884-372-0
ISSN 0383-5405

*En vente en français
sous le même titre*

PRINTED IN CANADA

Available from
your local bookstore;
the National Gallery bookstore;
or from National Museums of Canada, Order Fulfilment,
Ottawa   K1A OM8

Contents

New Young
Toronto Artist Paints
Subjective Group

Human Soul, Is Not Pink as Some
Psychiatrists Say, But Only the Artist
Himself Can Paint It –
Says His Only Subject Was His
Own Feeling.

Bertram Brooker's first exhibition is documented by an article in the *Toronto Star* of 5 February 1927 headed with the words you read at the top of this page. The article itself is unusual. Brooker (whose exhibition it records) is never named. The location of the exhibition (the Arts & Letters Club in Toronto) is not mentioned. Remarks of viewers are quoted anonymously. The strict rule of the club, that no event was to be publicly reported, had led to another strange newspaper article some fourteen years earlier. Then the spectacular activities of the "Hot Mush School" had to be brought to public attention. Bertram Brooker's first exhibition created a similar stir in the club, a club whose membership still, as fourteen

years before, touched virtually every significant artist in the city. Yet only three years later Brooker turned away from these pioneering experiments in abstraction.

Pioneering experiments they were, in Canada; and in Canada, at that time, they could only have reached even such brief a flowering in Toronto. Winnipeg, contrary to Russel Harper's contention that it was some kind of precocious hot-bed of abstraction,[1] only incidentally enters the story before these first experiments had been set aside. Born in Croydon, outside of London, England, in 1888, Brooker emigrated to Canada with his family early in 1905 and settled in Portage la Prairie. Just turned seventeen, he worked first with his father as a labourer on the Grand Trunk Pacific, but soon advanced through evening study to a clerical position. After six or seven years with the railway, he and a brother took over operation of the movie theatre in Neepawa, a small town northeast of Brandon, Manitoba. Inspired by

1 J. Russell Harper, *Painting in Canada: A History* (Toronto: University of Toronto Press, 1966). See "Towards Non-Objectivity," p. 351 ff.

the films, Bertram began to experiment with his own ideas, and in 1912 sold some detective-"thriller" scripts to Vitagraph, one of the larger American film-production companies. There was no creative future in film in Neepawa, Manitoba, however, and in 1914 Brooker returned to Portage la Prairie to work for the local newspaper. Following a stint in the Canadian Engineers during the war, he worked for newspapers in Winnipeg and Regina, and finally moved to Toronto in 1921 to become the editor of *Marketing*, then the trade journal of the Canadian advertising industry. He purchased the magazine in 1924; but by 1926 he had sold the business, evidently seeking the creative latitude that free-lance journalism could provide. That decision probably changed the course of his life.

Brooker could hardly have chosen a better moment. From early in 1926 until the great stock-market crash late in the fall of 1929, Toronto enjoyed an unprecedented series of art events both excellent and various. Much of this activity radiated from the energetic potency of the Group of Seven, then at the very peak of its influence in the more advanced art circles of the city. Brooker could not have avoided being touched by this creative fervour, and in fact seems to have sought its fundamental sources.

The pervasive influence of the Group of Seven on Canadian art in the thirties, and even forties, took two principal forms. The more obvious, as encountered in the work of such artists as A.J. Casson, Yvonne McKague Housser, Kathleen and George Pepper, Carl Schaefer, and a horde of earnest workers, has been called "Canadian Scene" painting. The term is not inappropriate, for many of these painters doubtless drew strength also from the parallel regional movement in the United States.

The other group influenced by the Seven is much smaller, their work more original, and consequently their early dependence on the Group less obvious. They drew on the "stance" of the Group; ideas rather than images. The artist who most attracted them was the one who himself was most concerned with ideas and with stance: Lawren Harris. It is not certain when Bertram Brooker met Harris. It was doubtless at the Arts & Letters Club at some point after Brooker joined. Harris himself was a charter member, and the club was still, in the later twenties, a "hang-out" for most of the Group of Seven (fig. 1).

Brooker began his first serious painting soon after meeting Harris. Among his papers are two documents that shed light on these beginnings. One consists of three typed pages headed "Extracts from *A Canadian Art Movement* by the famous author F.B. Housser." Housser's landmark book on the Group of Seven appeared in 1926, and one can assume that Brooker's notes date from shortly after that. He has transcribed some of Housser's remarks on the strength of the amateur movement in Canadian painting (Housser was, in 1929, to write on this subject again for Brooker's first yearbook), and has noted a number of his statements concerning the imminent burgeoning of artistic activity in Canada. But possibly most important of all, at that moment, he has transcribed some of Housser's remarks concerning the nature of spiritual growth.

Fred Housser was a prominent member of the Toronto Theosophical Society, as was Lawren Harris, and many of their ideas concerning the spiritual aspects of making or looking at art grew from their reading in theosophy. Brooker was aware of this, and doubtless was encouraged to pursue such a direction in his own life and with his own creative work. And an even stronger encouragement than Housser's popular defence of the Group of Seven existed in Lawren Harris's brilliant "Revelation of Art in Canada," which appear-

2 Lawren Harris, "Revelation of Art in Canada," *The Canadian Theosophist*, vol. VII, no. 5 (15 July 1926), pp. 85–88.
3 *Ibid.*, p. 85.

Fig. 1

In the Arts & Letters Club, Toronto, 1929.
From the left, Bertram Brooker, A.Y. Jackson,
Merrill Dennison, J.E.H. MacDonald,
Lawren Harris, Fred Housser, Arthur Lismer.
Photo by John Vanderpant

ed in *The Canadian Theosophist,* the organ of the Toronto Theosophical Society, in July 1926.[2] Brooker's personal copy is still among his papers.

Harris's eloquent presentation of his "views of the underlying principles of the movement which the Group of Seven represents"[3] would certainly have thrilled Brooker, who in 1926 was beginning to discover his own potential in painting. Harris's main points repeat precisely those Brooker had culled from Housser: the accelerating accumulation of creative energy drawing more and more people to painting, making it the most "Canadian" of art forms; the preeminence of honest native expression over imported art; and, most important, the conscious pursuit of spiritual qualities. The artist, "because of his constant habit of awareness and his discipline in expression, is perhaps more understanding of [Canada's] moods and spirit than others are. He is thus better equipped to interpret it to others, and then, when he has become one with the spirit, to create living works in their own right by using forms, colour, rhythms and moods, to make a harmonious home for the imaginative and spiritual meanings it has evoked in him."[4] Such a position called for a rendition not of the Canadian scene, but of the Canadian soul.

The last part of Harris's statement could describe in general terms one of Brooker's abstractions, but it could hardly by itself have stimulated their invention. The *idea* of abstract painting had, then, to come from somewhere else. The most likely single source is one of the great fountainheads of the modern western tradition: Wassily Kandinsky's *Über das Geistige in der Kunst* (Concerning the Spiritual in Art). Harper has noted the connection, but set it impossibly early in Brooker's life.[5] It surely was Lawren Harris who, probably after the publication of his own first extended statement concerning the place of spiritualism in art in

1926, turned Brooker to Kandinsky.[6] Brooker was deeply touched by Kandinsky's suggestion that one should consider abstract painting as one would music. Some of the works in his first exhibition – sponsored by Arthur Lismer at the Arts & Letters Club, in January of 1927 – were described by Brooker himself as "expressions of musical feeling; one a direct interpretation of a mood suggested by the Largo of Dvorak's New World Symphony."[7]

No list of the works exhibited in January 1927 has come down to us. We can speculate that *Abstraction – Music* (pl. 4) is one, and that *Toccata* (pl. 2), with its musical title, would have been included. Neither seems to have been drawn from direct experience of Kandinsky's paintings. They are rather literal translations of musical "shape": a solid mass of interlocking forms enclosing a space within which play individually-defined forms (as in *Toccata*) or suggestive, faceted planes (as in *Abstraction – Music*). With these first works, Brooker appears to have drawn images from within himself rather than from the world of art.

Like all painters, however, Brooker lived to look at art, and in 1927 he would have seen some of the most advanced painting of the day when the collection of the Société Anonyme (a foundation established to collect and promote the most advanced "modern" painting in the world) was exhibited at the Art Gallery of Toronto. Not all of the artists were new to him. He visited New York regularly at least once a year after moving east. Late in 1924, for instance, he purchased a work from the American abstract painter A.S. Baylinson.[8] Later, in January of 1929, he visited the Memorial Exhibition of the works of Raymond Duchamp-Villon at the Brummer Gallery in New York.[9] His annotated copy of the catalogue is still with his papers. Duchamp-Villon would have held special interest for Brooker. Two of his

---

4 *Ibid.,* p. 86.
5 Harper, *op. cit.,* p. 352. Harper relates a story of Brooker "somehow or somewhere during those railroading years" hearing of Kandinsky and being so taken with the subject that his workmates called him "Little Kandinsky." This could not have been possible. Brooker had left the railroad by 1912, the year Kandinsky's book was published, in German. It appeared in its first English edition only in 1914, entitled *The Art of Spiritual Harmony.* It is very unlikely Brooker could have seen it until after the war.

6 William Hart has set out Harris's relationship to Kandinsky's theories in "Theory and Practice of Abstract Art 1932–1948," *Lawren Harris Retrospective Exhibition, 1963* (Ottawa: The National Gallery of Canada, 1963), pp. 27–40.
7 "New Young Toronto Artist Paints Subjective Group," *Toronto Star*, 5 February 1927.
8 A.S. Baylinson to Brooker, 25 January 1925. Baylinson (1882–1950) was then secretary of the Society of Independent Artists, New York.

Fig. 2

Raymond Duchamp-Villon (1876–1918)
Baudelaire 1911
Terra-cotta
39.4 cm high
Art Gallery of Ontario, Toronto.
Given in memory of Harold Murchison Tovell
and Ruth Massey Tovell by their sons.

Toronto friends, Dr Harold and Ruth Tovell, collected the work of the French sculptor and owned at least two important pieces: *A Seated Girl (Jeune fille assise)* of 1914,[10] and the terra-cotta version of the famous *Baudelaire* of 1911 (fig. 2).[11] The latter impressed Brooker greatly, and at least two works of 1927 show its clear influence. The Tovells acquired one of these, *The Dawn of Man* (pl. 6). Its simplified and symbolic forms would have appealed to admirers of Duchamp-Villon.

The Tovells held regular "evenings" throughout the late twenties and early thirties, gatherings attended by the more sophisticated members of Toronto's cultural community; and it was from this group that the major support to book the Société Anonyme exhibition would have derived. Lawren Harris, nonetheless, was the single essential proponent of the exhibition. Harris was a friend of Katherine Dreier, New York patron of (among others) Mondrian, Kandinsky, and Duchamp – and President of the Société Anonyme. Harris was the only Canadian represented in the collection of the Société, although he chose not to exhibit with them in Toronto. Apparently, he brought such force to bear on the Toronto gallery to accept the exhibition that he felt it would appear self-seeking if his own work was then included. He exhibited as a member at the two other centres on the tour.

The exhibition was the first ever to introduce abstract art to Canada.[12] Expecting prejudice, Harris took pains to arrange a serious, positive press-conference; to have Miss Dreier give an introductory lecture at the opening; and personally to conduct interested persons around the exhibition. He later wrote an article stressing the importance of the show for Toronto.[13] His efforts were largely successful. Although there was no massive turning to the modern idiom, there were reasonable, interested articles in the newspapers and a minimum of

abuse. The only nasty invective was flung by Franz Johnston, the ex-member of the Group of Seven, who was invited to write against Harris.[14]

The Société Anonyme show – coming as it did only two months after his own first exhibition of abstract paintings – must greatly have encouraged Brooker. The Toronto art scene was definitely moving into a new phase. Because of the international attention given to the Group of Seven, creative, exploratory painting had been finally associated with ideas of quality among a relatively large group of viewers. The Ontario Society of Artists exhibition in March had been taken over by what the newspapers delightedly called "radical" artists! Brooker exhibited two works, including *Endless Dawn* (pl. 3). An even more exciting innovation appeared during the Art Gallery exhibition of Modern Art: the Simpson Galleries sponsored a *No-Jury Exhibition*.[15] Again the newspapers reacted with delight. They believed the contributing painters to be free of the restraint of having to pass a jury; better able to express deeper, more honest feelings. Brooker again showed two works, including *The Way* (pl. 7).

In 1928, he was asked to exhibit with the Group of Seven at their February showing.[16] He contributed two works, including the stunning *Sounds Assembling* (pl. 9; cover). He showed only pen-and-ink drawings at the O.S.A. that year; but the following March, he was represented by three magnificent abstractions, including *Alleluiah* (pl. 10) and *Resolution* (pl. 11), as well as by a special section devoted to forty of his pen-and-ink drawings. In 1930, he showed no abstractions, but in March of 1931 held a small retrospective of his abstractions at Hart House, in the University of Toronto (fig. 3). These were the last pure abstract oils he was to exhibit for sixteen years.

Why? As one would expect, there were

9   Raymond Duchamp-Villon (1876–1918).
10   George Heard Hamilton and William C. Agee, *Raymond Duchamp-Villon, 1876–1918* (New York: Walker and Company, 1967), pp. 84–86, repr. p. 85. Collection of Vincent Tovell, Toronto.
11   *Ibid.*, pp. 56–60. Collection of Art Gallery of Ontario, Toronto.
12   Toronto, Art Gallery of Toronto, 1–24 April 1927, *International Exhibition of Modern Art, Assembled by The Société Anonyme*. There is a catalogue with an introduction by Katherine Dreier.

13   Lawren Harris, "Modern Art and Aesthetic Reactions, An Appreciation," *The Canadian Forum*, vol. VII, no. 80 (May 1927), pp. 239–241.
14   Franz Johnston, "Modern Art and Aesthetic Reactions, An Objection," *The Canadian Forum*, vol. VII, no. 80 (May 1927), pp. 241–242.
15   Toronto, Simpson Galleries, 9–23 April 1927, *No-Jury Exhibition by Toronto Artists*. There is a catalogue with an anonymous foreword.

Fig. 3

Exhibition of Abstractions by Bertram Brooker,
Hart House Sketch Room, University of Toronto,
14 – 30 March 1931

many reasons. There continued to be a considerable amount of criticism levelled at abstraction, and, even worse, a belief among people he respected that abstraction was interesting but somehow unnatural in Canada, or at least untimely. "Abstraction is not a natural form of art expression in Canada," wrote the *Canadian Forum* critic in May 1930.[17] Reviewing the O.S.A. exhibition of 1927, the *Canadian Bookman*, which had consistently supported the Group of Seven, remarked that Brooker's contributions "are symbolic, mystical pictures which are difficult to appreciate."[18] Two years later the *Bookman* reviewer found Brooker's oils "interesting," but for her, Brooker conveyed "his maximum effect in black and white."[19] And although he exhibited with the Group of Seven in their last three shows (1928, 1930, 1931), he contributed abstractions only the first year, 1928. Harris and Lismer each sponsored him in one-man exhibitions, but MacDonald attacked him so severely at the time of his Arts & Letters Club début that he later wrote a long letter of apology. Sorry that he might have hurt Brooker's feelings, he nonetheless still felt the works "admirable . . . mostly as *design & Color*."[20]

Of course Brooker, as all pioneers, expected difficulties. Unlike most of the painters around him, however, he had other creative outlets, and these found ready acceptance when his painting did not. From 20 October 1928 until 15 November 1930 he wrote a regular newspaper column on artistic activity – painting, literature, theatre, etc. – in Canada, called "The Seven Arts," which was syndicated in five Southam newspapers across the country. Using the pseudonym Richard Surrey, Brooker wrote two technical manuals on advertising lay-out and copywriting which were published in New York in 1929 and 1930. Also in 1929, another New York firm published a special edition of excerpts from the Book of Kings called *Elijah*,

fully illustrated by Brooker (pls 15–17). Probably most important, however, was the *Yearbook of the Arts in Canada, 1928–1929* which he edited for Macmillan, and for which he wrote a lengthy and thoughtful introduction entitled "When We Awake," and an article on new Canadian sculpture. Everyone found his energy remarkable (fig. 4).

Although this variety of outlets clearly allowed him to leave his painting problems alone for long stretches, he probably would have returned to them with more relish if it had not been for the stock-market crash and Depression. Late in 1930 he found it necessary to seek a regular job once again after four years of creative freedom. He took a position with J.J. Gibbons, a Toronto-based advertising firm with interests in New York, London, and every major Canadian city – including Winnipeg. That proved to be one of the happier advantages of the job, for in the summer of 1929, Brooker had met LeMoine FitzGerald of Winnipeg. He was probably the single most powerful reason for the subsequent shift in Brooker's art.

Although Brooker had lived in Winnipeg for some years before moving to Toronto, and had always considered himself a "Winnipeger," he had not known FitzGerald prior to 1929. They then spent only two or three evenings together; but by December, Brooker had realized that his art would never again be the same. He had totally abandoned the painting of abstractions. Describing the repercussions of the visit, he wrote to FitzGerald that "so far its effect has been that I have become perhaps too realistic – in a small way, I mean – but I hope to grow out of that to a bigger appreciation of form – particularly."[21] The only mention of abstract art in the first few letters between the two was in FitzGerald's reply to Brooker's first letter of December: "I fear your conversation had a very definite effect on Edward.

16   Toronto, Art Gallery of Toronto, February 1928, *Canadian Paintings by the Group of Seven*. There is a catalogue.
17   *The Canadian Forum*, vol. x, no. 116 (May 1930), p. 288.
18   "O.S.A. Exhibition," *The Canadian Bookman*, vol. ix, no. 3 (March 1927), p. 78.
19   Jeanne Adeney, "Art Notes," *The Canadian Bookman*, vol. xi, no. 4 (April 1929), p. 99.
20   MacDonald to Brooker, 28 January 1927.

Fig. 4

Arthur Lismer (1885–1969)
The Brooker Quartettttte! *c*. 1930
Charcoal
23.7 × 30.2 cm
Estate of M.A. Brooker

His Christmas card was a very abstract thing . . . ."[22] Edward, FitzGerald's son, was then thirteen years old.

This radical change did not strike so deep as first might appear. In March of 1930 he exhibited his *Danish Urn* (pl. 20) in the O.S.A. annual exhibition; and the next month he chose to display, with the Group of Seven, a work entitled *Landscape* that has not survived, and the striking *Snow Fugue* (pl. 21). (*Snow Fugue* was shown again later that year at the Canadian National Exhibition.) Though he had turned away from an abstract idiom, he sought obviously to achieve the same end with his new realism. *Snow Fugue* is in formal terms similar to *Striving* (pl. 19), for instance, and its musical title encourages such an abstract approach to the viewing of the painting. It was on such ground that Brooker and FitzGerald could meet.

That they continued to meet was very important to Brooker. "I got so attached to you while you were here that I'd hate to go for a long stretch of months or a year without some contact with you,"[23] he wrote after a visit Fitz-Gerald had been persuaded to make to Toronto during the summer of 1930. They were fortunate if they saw one another once a year, however; but they wrote regularly, and the correspondence that has been saved is rich with the fruits of a friendship that extended almost to the end of both their lives. FitzGerald died only a bit more than a year after Brooker.

Brooker was profoundly influenced by FitzGerald's art (*Williamson's Garage* is a typical example of the Winnipeg artist's work at about the time of the meeting[24]), but was even more strongly drawn to the man himself. He ceaselessly promoted FitzGerald's interests in the East, encouraged Lawren Harris and other Group members to take an interest in him (which led to FitzGerald's being formally included as a member of the Group of Seven in

1932), and fed him with a constant flow of Toronto art-gossip in an attempt to counteract what he felt to be the oppressive insularity of Winnipeg in the thirties. FitzGerald responded with warmth and respect, and in his last years even tried his hand at a few abstractions – more than twenty years after Brooker's first encouragements.

Coincidental with this developing friendship, Brooker became more critical of the Group of Seven, describing their diminishing abilities in his letters, and even, after the 1930 show, foretelling their dissolution. "It marked the death-knell of the Group of Seven as an organization," he wrote.[25] He was unknowingly reflecting a view held by artists all over Canada in the early thirties. Like many, however, Brooker found himself still drawn to the basic formula developed by the Group, and during the summer of 1931 he even visited the region around Murray Bay in Quebec at the encouragement of Jackson and Harris. Upon his return to Toronto, he worked up one of the sketches into *The St. Lawrence* (pl. 27), and later that year exhibited it in the last Group of Seven exhibition. Harris, doubtless uncomfortable in recognizing its relationship to his own austere canvases of Lake Superior or the Rockies, criticized the trees.[26]

Brooker didn't seem to care. *The St. Lawrence* was completely overshadowed by a work he had completed for the O.S.A. exhibition earlier that year which had isolated him from many of the artists in Toronto he had considered his supporters. This was his *Figures in Landscape* (pl. 26) which, after having been accepted by the O.S.A. jury for inclusion in the 1931 show, was removed from the exhibition and from the catalogue by officers of the Art Gallery of Toronto. It was even claimed in one report that it was questioning by Arthur Lismer, who directed the children's art programme, that had led to its removal.[27] Though

---

21   Brooker to FitzGerald, 28 December 1929.
22   FitzGerald to Brooker, 11 January 1930.
23   Brooker to FitzGerald, 17 October 1930.
24   Oil on canvas, 55.9 × 45.7 cm. Collection of The National Gallery of Canada. Published in R.H. Hubbard, *The National Gallery of Canada, Catalogue of Paintings and Sculpture*, volume III: Canadian School (Ottawa: The National Gallery of Canada, 1960), repr. p. 84. *Williamson's Garage* was painted early in 1927, and was exhibited in the O.S.A. that year. It is probably the first FitzGerald

Brooker would have seen. The National Gallery purchased the work in 1929.
25   Brooker to FitzGerald, 27 November 1931.
26   Brooker to FitzGerald, 10 January 1932.

Brooker was described as a "follower" of the Group of Seven in newspaper articles, none of the Group appears to have publicly supported him.

Although figures, clothed or not, seldom appeared in Group of Seven exhibitions, Brooker had the right to expect some support. Only the year before, Edwin Holgate, a *bona fide* Group member, had exhibited his *Nude in a Landscape* in the National Gallery of Canada Annual.[28] Brooker even followed Holgate's lead in placing his figures in a stylized landscape setting. But rather than Holgate, he should have remembered John Russell, the Toronto society artist, whose painting of a nude at the C.N.E. in 1927 stirred up great controversy and stimulated the displeasure of (among others) Lawren Harris.[29] In 1931, Brooker did receive support from Dorothy Stevens,[30] who also exhibited paintings of nude women. And he wrote very ably in his own defence, typically cutting to the heart of the problem with frankness: sexuality, naturally one of the primary concerns of the creative man, is in Anglo-Saxon culture thwarted and perverted and finally destroyed. The men who removed his painting from the Art Gallery walls to "save" the children were futilely trying to protect them from a monster they themselves had created, and were in fact strengthening by their very action. Brooker's article appeared in a relatively obscure anthology, too late in the year to have much of a response.[31] In August he wrote FitzGerald: "I have been working on another nude and will probably have it finished for the Group show, but whether the Group fellows will want to accept it, I don't know."[32] He showed only *Still Life* and *St. Lawrence.*

Brooker neither turned from nor faltered in his course. His writing, as always, took up most of the time his job as an advertising executive left free; and that was very little. He continued to experiment (with portraits, still lifes, landscapes) and to think, and to discuss with FitzGerald the goals and shortcomings of his art. One of the great shortcomings, they both would have agreed, was that Brooker had not enough time to devote to the hard work of painting. Time and again he complains, in his letters, of being torn from his painting by the demands of advertising clients. At first he thought that by writing commercial fiction he could make enough money to return to freelancing. That, however, wouldn't necessarily give him more time for painting. Finally, in the spring of 1934, he was able to make an arrangement with J.J. Gibbons whereby he worked only four days per week with a commensurate cut in salary. Brooker was delighted, and the years from 1934 to 1937 are, with the abstract period from 1927 to 1930, the most prolific, coherent, and generally successful of his whole painting career. Paintings such as *Phyllis* (pl. 31), *Fawn Bay* (pl. 35), *Ski Poles* (pl. 36), and the startling *Torso* (pl. 42), are penetrating in their realism, dynamic in composition, and harmonious in colour and texture. Any debt Brooker owed FitzGerald was generously repaid with interest in the original conception underlying the bulk of these works.

This partial liberation from his advertising office was only part of the reason for the great success he enjoyed between 1934 and 1937. In November of 1933, the first Toronto exhibition of the Canadian Group of Painters (C.G.P.) was held. Brooker was one of the more enthusiastic of the charter members, and actively supported the Group's programme until at least the mid-forties. He understood the new group initially as an attempt on the part of the Group of Seven to associate themselves with a broader, more vital segment of the art community in Canada:

The Group, in other words, recognized that it has passed the peak of production. J.E.H. has

---

27 "Nudes in Landscape' Causes Art Dispute," *Toronto Star*, 7 March 1931.
28 Oil on canvas 73.7 × 116.9 cm. Collection of The National Gallery of Canada. Published in Hubbard, *op. cit.*, repr. p. 129. It was purchased that same year by the National Gallery.
29 Lawren Harris, "The Nudes at the C.N.E.," *The Canadian Forum*, vol. VIII, no. 85 (1927), pp. 391–392. John Wentworth Russel (1879–1959).
30 Dorothy Stevens Austin (1888–1966).
31 Bertram Brooker, "Nudes and Prudes," in *Open House* (Ottawa: Graphic Publishers Limited, 1931), pp. 93–106.
32 Copy of Brooker to FitzGerald, 6 August 1931.

been very ill lately, and in any case, even if he recovers full strength, will probably not do much more painting. Varley was seriously ill this past summer and is very hard up, I hear.... He had only one canvas in the show.... Casson scarcely counted at all, and Carmichael had only about two things which were very reminiscent of stuff done five years ago. Lismer's Maritime canvases were hurried and rather literal. They did not excite anyone very much. Jackson showed up best of all with a lot of things along his usual line. Lawren has done no painting for six months and very little for a year.... The general impression, freely voiced, seems to be that he is repeating himself and has got to the end – of a phase, at least. Holgate has had to concentrate on commercial work and consequently had only two small portraits to show, neither of them very exceptional. [33]

For the next few years Brooker felt himself in league with the more advanced painters in the country who had plucked the torch of Canadian art from failing hands, and were racing it on in new directions, to new successes.

In the period 1936–37 there was again, as in the period 1929–30, a great surge in all the fields of Brooker's activity. Five years of writing culminated in the publication of his first novel, *Think of the Earth*, which in 1936 won the first Governor-General's Award for Fiction. That same year he published a mystery novel under a pseudonym, and the second *Yearbook of the Arts in Canada* appeared. In 1937 he held two one-man exhibitions, one in April at Douglas Duncan's Picture Loan Society, and the other in November at Hart House, in the University of Toronto. His previous one-man show had been held there six years earlier.

He had mentioned to FitzGerald, some years before, that "after this apprenticeship to natur-

alistic painting has been served a little more fully I shall perhaps go back to more abstract things with a greater command of mediums and do something quite different." [34] Late in 1937 he did something very close to that, and exhibited two of the results in the C.G.P. exhibition that November. Neither *Blue Nude* (pl. 41) nor *Entombment* (pl. 43) are really abstractions like those of the late twenties. They are rather stylizations; plays on cubist compositional devices; symbolic figures. Although monumental, ambitious canvases, they seem, at this remove, to lack the vitality of his earlier work.

Brooker switched to the MacLaren Advertising Company in November of 1940, and remained there for the rest of his working years, holding the position of vice-president at his retirement. His role there obviously demanded much of his time, and the quantity of his painting began to taper off. He no longer exhibited so much, or so often, in the society exhibitions; and although he held three one-man shows during the forties, his major canvases of that period do not grow out of a coherent, related body of work.

There are exceptions. From around the period 1941–42 date a group of landscapes of clarity and beauty that display a concern to paint reflectively. But his tendency was to work up a limited number of "show-piece" paintings of great visual impact, lacking, to some degree, the richer complexities and subtleties that arise from working on a number of related pieces over an extended period. Many of the paintings of the forties, notably *Pharaoh's Daughter* (pl. 59), are in fact reworkings of earlier essays. Interestingly enough, most of these later works display a closed composition rather than the open, expanding composition of the paintings of the late twenties and thirties.

Paul Duval once remarked that Brooker disproved the old adage that "art and business

---

33   Brooker to FitzGerald, 10 January 1932.   34   Brooker to FitzGerald, 26 March 1931.

cannot mix."[35] Unfortunately, Duval was wrong. It is clear that Brooker was most successful when he was best able to separate his art from his business. Those of us who greatly admire the notable successes and who are thrilled by the dynamic, creative energies of the man, must regret that he was unable to find a way to make his art his only business.

35 Paul Duval, "A Man Remembered," Toronto *Telegram*, 18 February 1956.

1

Creation *c*. 1927
Oil on board
60.9 × 43.2 cm
Private collection

2

Toccata c. 1927
Oil on board
60.9 × 43.2 cm
Estate of M.A. Brooker

3

Endless Dawn   1927
Oil on board
43.2 × 60.9 cm
Estate of M.A. Brooker

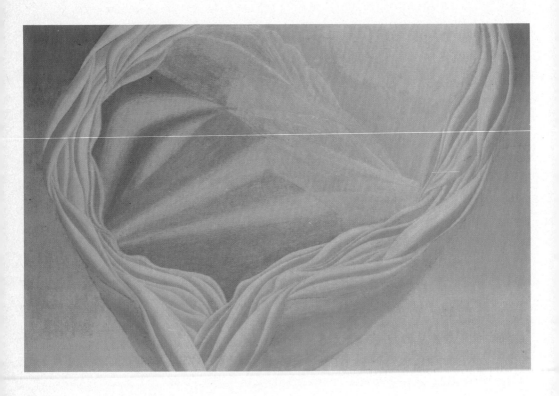

4

Abstraction – Music   *c*. 1927
Oil on board
43.2 × 60.9 cm
London Regional Art Gallery, London, Ontario
F.B. Housser Memorial Collection

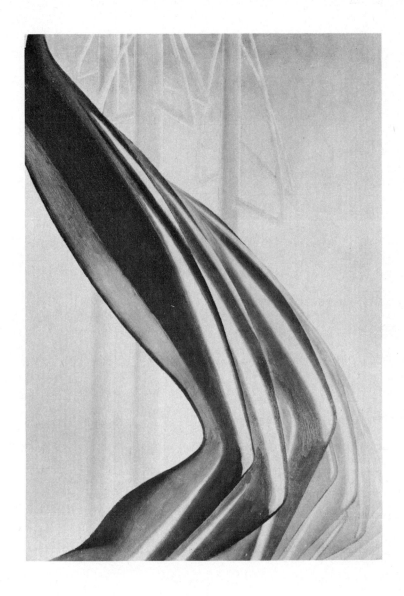

5

Green Movement *c.* 1927
Oil on board
60.9 × 43.2 cm
Art Gallery of Ontario, Toronto
Purchased with assistance from Wintario, 1978

6

The Dawn of Man   *c*. 1927
Oil on canvas
112.4 × 81.3 cm
National Gallery of Canada, Ottawa
Presented in memory of Harold and
Ruth Tovell by their four sons, 1972

7

8

7

8

The Way   1927
Oil on canvas
59.7 × 74.9 cm
Mrs David Koerner, Vancouver

"Energy is Eternal Delight" – Blake   1927
Reprinted from *Canadian Forum*,
vol. VIII, no 85 (October 1927), p. 403

9

Sounds Assembling   1928
Oil on canvas
113.0 × 91.4 cm
Winnipeg Art Gallery
Purchased 1945

10

Alleluiah 1929
Oil on canvas
122.2 × 121.9 cm
National Gallery of Canada, Ottawa
Purchased 1969

11

Resolution   1929–30
Oil on canvas
60.9 × 76.2 cm
Ms Diana Waddington, Vancouver

12

Ascending Forms   *c*. 1929
Oil on canvas
76.2 × 61.3 cm
National Gallery of Canada, Ottawa
Purchased 1969

13

Evolution *c*. 1929
Oil on canvas
76.5 × 61.3 cm
National Gallery of Canada, Ottawa
Purchased 1969

14

Geometric Forms   1930
Pen, black ink on paper
36.5 × 27.94 cm
National Gallery of Canada, Ottawa
Gift of Mr Victor Brooker, Toronto, 1970

15

I Kings, XXI, 26   c. 1929
Reprinted from *Elijah*
(New York: William Edwin Rudge, 1929)

16

II Kings, II, 11   *c*. 1929
Reprinted from *Elijah*
(New York: William Edwin Rudge, 1929)

17

I Kings, XIX, 13   c. 1929
Reprinted from *Elijah*
(New York: William Edwin Rudge, 1929)

18

"Head" *c*. 1930
Oil on canvas
60.9 × 50.8 cm
Estate of M.A. Brooker

19

Striving c. 1930
Oil on canvas
76.2 × 60.9 cm
Dr Leonard Gazen, Toronto

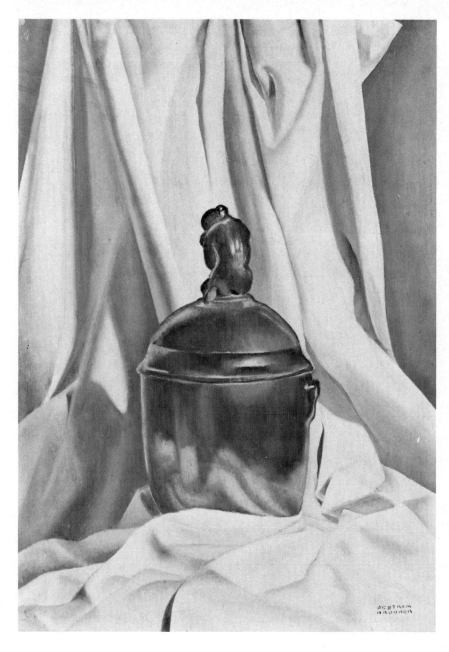

20

Danish Urn   1930
Oil on canvas
43.2 × 60.9 cm
Mrs Doreen Fast, Sunnyvale, California, U.S.A.

21

Snow Fugue 1930
Oil on canvas
101.6 × 101.6 cm
Royal Conservatory of Music, Toronto
Mazzoleni Collection

22

23

22

23

Fever (Crime and Punishment)   1930
Pen and ink on paper
28.3 × 20.7 cm (image)
Art Gallery of Ontario, Toronto
Purchased 1943

Realization (Crime and Punishment)   1930
Pen and ink on paper
28.3 × 20.5 cm (image)
Art Gallery of Ontario, Toronto
Purchased 1943

24

Maple Stump, Avenue Road   1931
Graphite on paper
30.5 × 42.5 cm
National Gallery of Canada, Ottawa
Gift of Dr Walter M. Tovell, Toronto, 1972

25

Maple in Beaverton Churchyard 1931
Graphite on paper
34.9 × 27.3 cm
Estate of M.A. Brooker

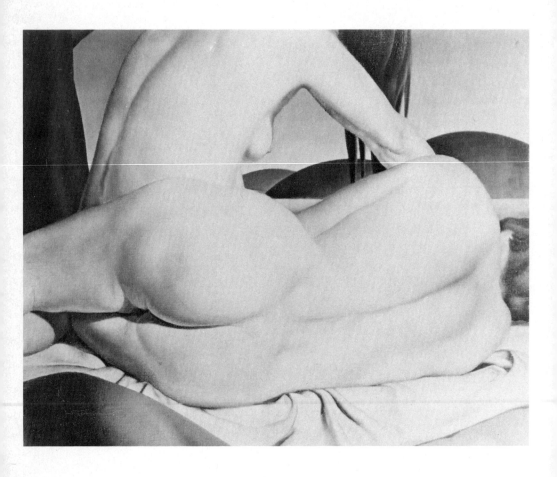

26

Figures in Landscape   1931
Oil on canvas
60.9 × 76.2 cm
Private collection

27

The St. Lawrence   1931
Oil on canvas
76.9 × 101.9 cm
National Gallery of Canada, Ottawa
Gift from the Douglas M. Duncan
Collection, 1970

28

Portrait of Morley Callaghan   1932
Oil on canvas
76.2 × 60.96 cm
Mr Morley Callaghan, Toronto

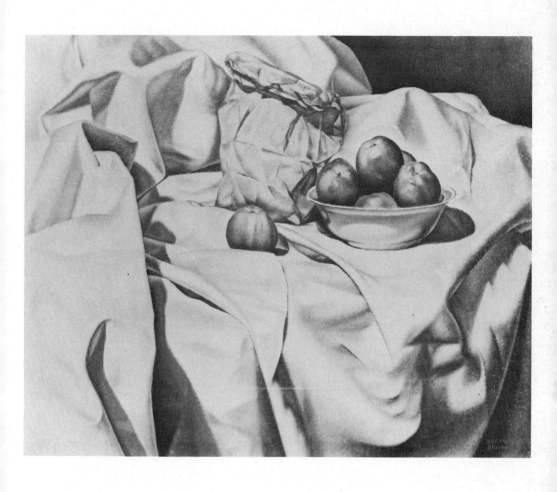

29

Still Life with Bag   1933
Oil on canvas
68.6 × 83.8 cm
Mrs Ellen Burtonshaw,
Portage la Prairie, Manitoba

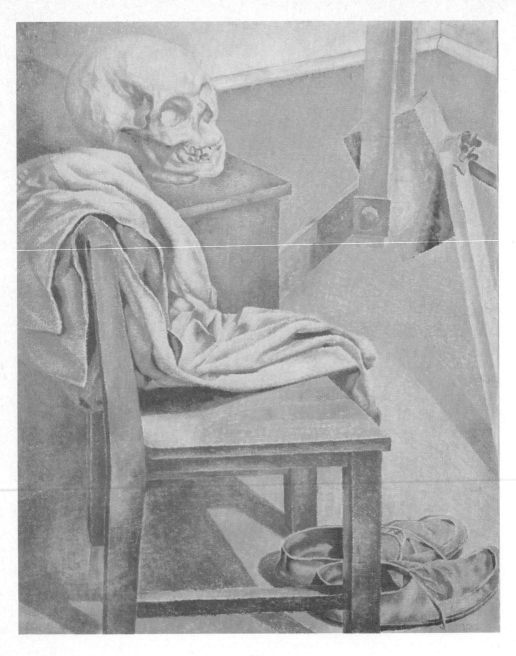

30

Art is Long 1934
Oil on canvas
76.2 × 60.9 cm
Estate of M.A. Brooker

31

Phyllis (Piano! Piano!)   1934
Oil on canvas
101.6 × 76.2 cm
Estate of M.A. Brooker

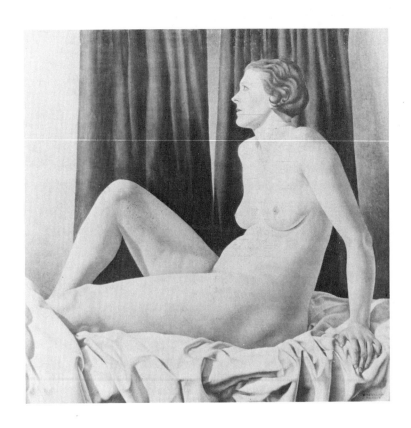

32

Seated Figure   1935
Oil on canvas
101.6 × 101.6 cm
Estate of M.A. Brooker

33

Through the Trees, Muskoka Lake   1936
Graphite on paper
35.56 × 25.4 cm
National Gallery of Canada, Ottawa
Gift of Mr Victor Brooker, Toronto, 1970

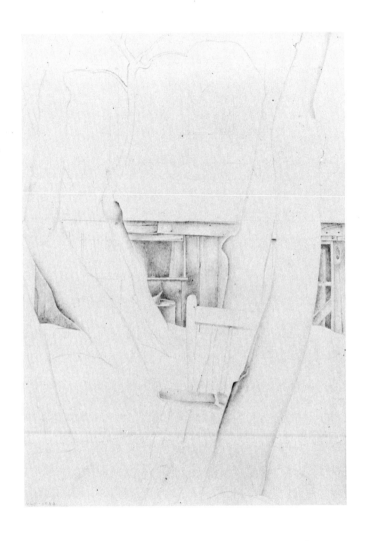

34

Backyard Study   1936
Graphite on paper
35.4 × 25.2 cm
Estate of M.A. Brooker

35

Fawn Bay　1936
Oil on canvas
60.9 × 76.2 cm
Mr and Mrs Dean Hughes, Unionville, Ontario

36

Ski Poles 1936
Oil on canvas
60.9 × 76.2 cm
Private collection

37

Caledon Hills   *c*. 1935
Oil on canvas
76.2 × 97.8 cm
Art Gallery of Ontario, Toronto
Purchased with funds from the
Estate of Mrs Helen Richardson Stearns, 1972

38

Marrow and Lemons   1937
Oil on canvas
45.7 × 60.9 cm
Mr and Mrs Max Merkur, Toronto

39

Cabbage and Pepper 1937
Oil on canvas
40.6 × 50.8 cm
Confederation Centre Art Gallery and Museum,
Charlottetown, Prince Edward Island
Purchased 1973

40

Three Figures   1937
Oil on canvas
96.5 × 53.3 cm
London Regional Art Gallery, London, Ontario
Purchased 1972

41

Blue Nude   1937
Oil on canvas mounted on masonite
101.6 × 50.8 cm
Mr Harold Gustafsson, Brampton, Ontario

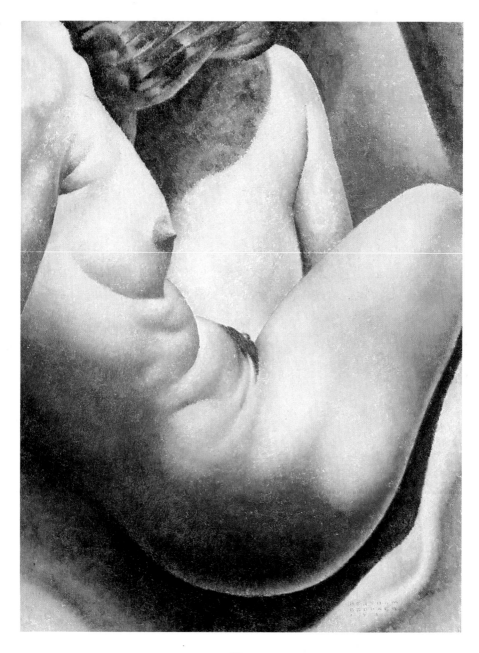

42

Torso 1937
Oil on canvas
61.6 × 45.7 cm
National Gallery of Canada, Ottawa
Purchased 1971

43

Entombment   1937
Oil on canvas
101.6 × 101.6 cm
Estate of M.A. Brooker

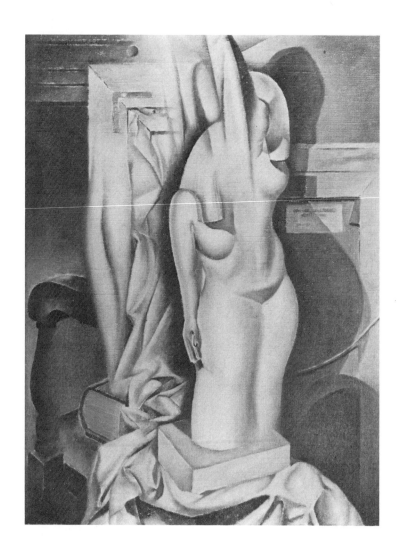

44

Egyptian Woman   c. 1939
Oil on canvas
50.9 × 45.7 cm
Mr Victor Brooker, Toronto

45

Pygmalion's Miracle   1940
Oil on canvas
97.8 × 53.3 cm
Estate of M.A. Brooker

46

Sandbanks, Picton   *c.* 1942
Oil on canvas
50.9 × 114.3 cm
Dr D.R. Yadav, Calgary

47

Quebec Impression c. 1942
Oil on canvas
96.5 × 76.2 cm
Estate of M.A. Brooker

48

The Cloud *c.* 1942
Oil on canvas
61.3 × 76.2 cm
National Gallery of Canada, Ottawa
Purchased 1969

49

North Shore   *c*. 1942
Oil on canvas
50.9 × 76.2 cm
Mr Charles Chandler, Montreal

50

Green Composition   1945
Watercolour
28.4 × 35.9 cm
Winnipeg Art Gallery
Purchased 1977

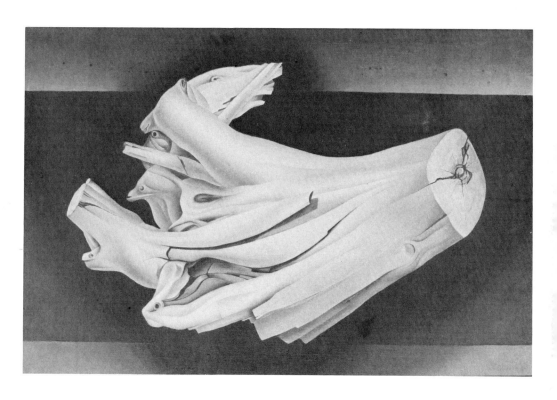

51

Driftwood   1945
Oil on canvas
66.0 × 100.3 cm
Mr Victor Brooker, Toronto

52

Symphonic Forms   *c*. 1945
Oil on canvas mounted on masonite
29.9 × 37.5 cm
The McMichael Canadian Collection,
Kleinburg, Ontario

53

Symphonic Forms   1947
Oil on canvas
69.8 × 92.7 cm
Estate of M.A. Brooker

54

Trees and Snow 1948
Oil on canvas
76.2 × 60.9 cm
Private collection

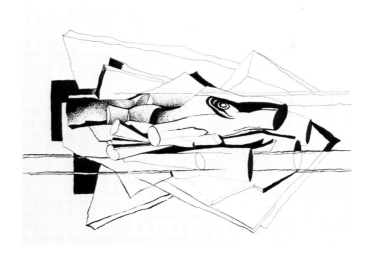

55

Study I, Progression *c*. 1948
Pen and ink on poster paper
24.1 × 34.3 cm
Art Gallery of Ontario, Toronto
Gift from the McLean Foundation, 1963

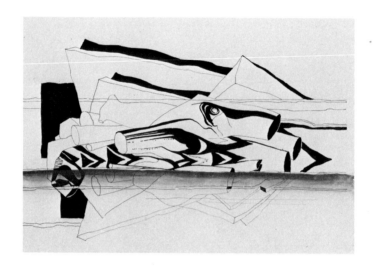

56

Study II, Progression *c*. 1948
Pen and ink on poster paper
24.0 × 34.1 cm
Art Gallery of Ontario, Toronto
Gift from the McLean Foundation, 1963

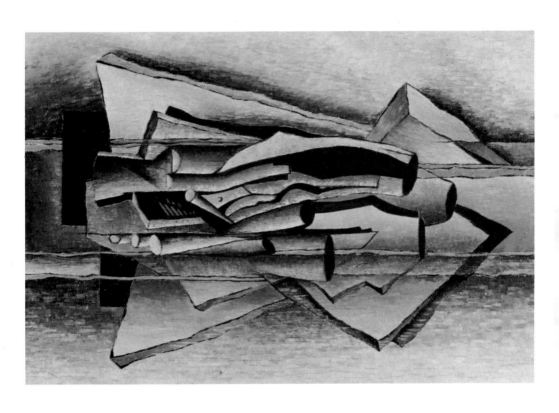

57

Progression   1948
Oil on canvas
66.0 × 99.7 cm
Art Gallery of Ontario, Toronto
Gift from the Albert H. Robson
Memorial Subscription Fund, 1948

58

Suspension 1949
Oil on canvas
99.1 × 69.8 cm
Mr and Mrs M. Sharf, Toronto

59

Pharaoh's Daughter   1950
Oil on canvas
99.1 × 66.0 cm
Private collection

Principal Exhibitions

1927

Toronto, The Arts & Letters Club, January 1927, *Bertram Brooker*.

REVIEW
"New Young Toronto Artist Paints Subjective Group," *Star* (Toronto), 5 February 1927.

1929

Toronto, The Art Gallery of Toronto, March 1929, *Drawings by Bertram Brooker*. A numbered check-list was published with an introduction by Lawren Harris.

REVIEW
Jeanne Adeney, "Art Notes," *The Canadian Bookman*, vol. XI, no. 4 (April 1929), p. 99.

1931

Toronto, Hart House Sketch Room, University of Toronto, 14–30 March 1931, *Bertram Brooker Abstractions,* There is partial photographic documentation (fig. 3).

1935

Toronto, The Galleries of J. Merritt Malloney, 18 May – 1 June 1935, *An Exhibition of Drawings by Kathleen Munn, LeMoine FitzGerald, Bertram Brooker*. A numbered check-list was published.

REVIEW
G. Campbell McInnes, "The World of Art," *Saturdy Night*, vol. L, no. 29 (25 May 1935), p. 11.

1937

Toronto, The Picture Loan Society, April 1937, *Bertram Brooker*.

REVIEW
G. Campbell McInnes, "The World of Art," *Saturday Night*, vol. LII, no. 22 (3 April 1937), p. 8.

Works mentioned: Drawings for "Crime and Punishment," A Corner of the Studio.
Toronto, Hart House Art Gallery, University of Toronto, November 1937, *Bertram Brooker*. There is a check-list.

1942

Toronto, Hart House Art Gallery, University of Toronto, January 1942, *Bertram Brooker*. There is a check-list.

1947

Toronto, The Arts & Letters Club, September 1947, *Bertram Brooker*. There is a numbered check-list.

1949

Toronto, Hart House Art Gallery, University of Toronto, from 7 November 1949, *Bertram Brooker*. There is a check-list.

REVIEWS

Graydon Bell, "Bertram Brooker," *The Varsity*, University of Toronto, 17 November 1949.

Pearl McCarthy, "Art and Artists," *Globe and Mail* (Toronto), 26 November 1949.

1956

Toronto, The Ontario Society of Artists, The Art Gallery of Toronto, 17 February–18 March 1956, *Bertram Brooker, O.S.A. (1885 [sic] –1955)*. A catalogue with an introduction by LeMoine FitzGerald was included in the catalogue of the eighty-fourth annual exhibition of the Ontario Society of Artists.

REVIEW

Paul Duval, "A Man Remembered," *Telegram* (Toronto), 18 February 1956.

1968

Toronto, The Arts & Letters Club, 21 October –15 November 1968, *Bertram Brooker*. There is a numbered check-list.

1970

Toronto, The Morris Gallery, 12–26 September 1970, *Bertram Brooker, 1888–1955, Drawings & Watercolours*.

REVIEWS

Paul Russell, "Canada's First Abstract Painter Featured in Special Exhibition," *Star* (Toronto), 12 September 1970.

Kay Kritzwiser, "At the Galleries," *Globe and Mail* (Toronto), 12 September 1970.

1971

Toronto, The Morris Gallery, 23 October–6 November 1971, *Bertram Brooker 1888–1955*. An illustrated catalogue was published.

1972

Circulating exhibition, National Gallery of Canada, 1972–1973, *Bertram Brooker, A Retrospective Exhibition*. A numbered check-list was published.

REVIEWS

"Sarnia Art Gallery to Feature Work of Bertram Brooker," *Sarnia Observer*, 6 November 1972.

"Wide Variation of Approach Seen in Bertram Brooker Show," *Sarnia Observer*, 29 November 1972.

1973

REVIEWS

Lenore Crawford, "Exhibit of Brooker Paintings 'Fine Tour' of 1927–50 Works," *London Free Press*, 16 January 1973.

Catherine Bates, "Past and Present," *Montreal Star*, 10 March 1973.

"Bertram Brooker Show in Winnipeg," *Daily Graphic* (Portage La Prairie), 6 July 1973.

Janice Keys, "Brooker's Son Says Father Met with Indifference Here," *Winnipeg Free Press*, 11 July 1973.

Jeremy Boultbee, "'Great Name' Artist on Display," *Victoria Times*, 14 September 1973.

Erith Smith, "Show Drips Realism," *Victoria Colonist*, 14 September 1973.

1974

Montreal, Galerie Jeanne Newman, from 16 November 1974, *Bertram Brooker*. An illustrated check-list was published.

1975

Winnipeg, Winnipeg Art Gallery, 31 January–13 April 1975, *Lionel LeMoine FitzGerald, Bertram Brooker, Their Drawings*. A catalogue was published, and the exhibition subsequently circulated.

REVIEWS

Patricia E. Bovey, "Two Artists Pioneers in Abstraction," *Winnipeg Free Press*, 25 January 1975.

James Purdie, "Opposites Attract in Unlikely Alliance," *Globe and Mail* (Toronto), 21 August 1976.

"Exhibition Compares Styles of Artists," *Ottawa Citizen*, 28 August 1976.

1976

Toronto, The Morris Gallery, 10–24 April 1976 [*Bertram Brooker*].

REVIEWS

Gary Michael Dault, "Brooker Exhibition Highly Recommended," *Star* (Toronto), 9 April 1976.

James Purdie, "Avery and Brooker Acclaimed at Last," *Globe and Mail* (Toronto), 24 April 1976.

1977

Toronto, The Morris Gallery, May 1977 [*Bertram Brooker*].

REVIEW

Gary Michael Dault, "Brooker Genius as the Artist on Show Again," *Star* (Toronto), 3 May 1977.

Halifax, Zwicker's Gallery, from 20 October 1977, *Bertram Brooker, 1888–1955*.

REVIEW

"Brooker Exhibition on at Zwicker's," *Halifax Chronicle Herald*, 20 October 1977.

1978

Paris, Ontario, The Homestead Gallery, 5–19 February 1978, *Bertram Brooker (1888–1955)*.

REVIEWS

Carol Ann Wilson, "Canadian Art on Display," *Brantford Expositor*, 4 February 1978.

David Moore, "Brooker Works May Be One-of-a-Kind Exhibit," *Brantford Expositor*, 15 February 1978.

Toronto, The Morris Gallery, 22 April–6 May 1978, *Brooker Estate*.

REVIEWS

Stephen Godfrey, "Verbs on Paper Give Action to the Eye," *Globe and Mail* (Toronto), 29 April 1978.

Gary Michael Dault, "Artist's Drawings Full of Energy," *Star* (Toronto), 1 May 1978.

1979

Winnipeg, Accents and Art Gallery, until 24 March 1979 [*Bertram Brooker*].

REVIEW

Leonard Marcoe, "Brooker Deserving of Fuller Show," *Winnipeg Free Press*, 10 March 1979.

Selected Bibliography

Brooker, Bertram, ed. *Yearbook of the Arts in Canada, 1928 –1929*. Toronto: Macmillan, 1929.

——. *Elijah*. New York: William Edwin Rudge, 1929.

Surrey, Richard [Bertram Brooker]. *Layout Technique in Advertising*. New York: McGraw-Hill, 1929.

——. *Copy Technique in Advertising*. New York: McGraw-Hill, 1930.

Brooker, Bertram. "Mysticism Debunked." *The Canadian Forum*, vol. x, no. 114 (March 1930), pp. 202 –203.

——. "Idolators of Brevity." *Sewanee Review*, vol. xxxix (July – September 1931), pp. 263 –268.

——. "Nudes and Prudes." In *Open House*. Ottawa: Graphic Publishers, 1931, pp. 93 –106.

——. "A Review of the Arts at the Canadian National Exhibition, 1932." *The Journal, Royal Architectural Institute of Canada*, vol. ix, no. 110 (October 1932), pp. 232 –234.

——. *Think of the Earth*. Toronto: Thomas Nelson, 1936.

Huxley Herne [Bertram Brooker]. *Tangled Miracle*. London: Thomas Nelson and Sons, 1936.

Brooker, Bertram, ed. *Yearbook of the Arts in Canada, 1936*. Toronto: Macmillan, 1936.

——. "A Scene from 'The Storks'." *Lamps* (winter 1938 –39), pp. 14 –17.

——. *The Robber*. Toronto: Collins, 1949.

Charlesworth, Hector. "Vision in Black and White." *Saturday Night*, vol. xlv, no. 14 (15 February 1930), p. 10.

FitzGerald, LeMoine. *Bertram Brooker, O.S.A. (1885*[sic]*–1955)*. Toronto: Art Gallery of Toronto, 1956. (Exhibition catalogue of the eighty-fourth annual exhibition of the Ontario Society of Artists.)

"Free Speech in Art." *The Canadian Forum*, vol. xi, no. 127 (April 1931), p. 245.

Harris, Lawren. *Pen and Ink Drawings–By Bertram Brooker*. Toronto: Art Gallery of Toronto, 1929. (Exhibition catalogue of the fifty-seventh annual exhibition of the Ontario Society of Artists.)

Lebourdais, D.M. "Protean." *Saturday Night*, vol. LXV, no. 30 (2 May 1950), p. 20.

Lee, Thomas R. "Bertram Brooker, 1888–1955." *Canadian Art*, vol. XIII, no. 3 (spring 1956), pp. 286–291.

Salinger, Jehanne Bietry. "The Work of Bertram Brooker." *The Canadian Forum*, vol. X, no. 117 (June 1930), pp. 331–332.

"Two Drawings by Bertram Brooker." *Maritime Art*, vol. II, no. 5 (July 1942), pp. 156–157.

Zemans, Joyce. "The Art and Weltanschauung of Bertram Brooker," *Artscanada*, nos 176/177 (February–March 1973), pp. 65–68.

IN THE NEWSPAPERS

Brooker contributed a regular column to the Southam chain of newspapers, "The Seven Arts," from 20 October 1928 until 15 November 1930.

Brooker, Bertram. "Letter to the Editor: Mr Brooker Replies." Winnipeg *Tribune*, 27 September 1929.

——. "Letter to the Editor: Mr Brooker Replies." Winnipeg *Tribune*, 12 December 1929.

——. "Letter to the Editor." *Winnipeg Free Press*, 7 April 1930.

Bridle, Augustus. "Brooker's Nude was Crated by Decision of Majority." Toronto *Star*, 14 March 1931.

Cunliffe, Guy S. "Nude Painting Sent to Cellar as Artists' Exhibition Opens Creating First-Rate Mystery." Toronto *Mail and Empire*, 7 March 1931.

G., R.D. "Letter to the Editor: Ban on Nudes." Toronto *Star*, 14 March 1931.

Pyper, C.B. "An Eastern Critic." Winnipeg *Tribune*, 17 September 1929.

" 'Nudes in Landscape' Causes Art Dispute." Toronto *Star*, 7 March 1931.

"Artist, Author, Advertising Man Won Fiction Prize." Obituary, Toronto *Globe and Mail*, 22 March 1955.

"Bertram Brooker." Obituary, Toronto *Globe and Mail*, 23 March 1955.

"Bertram Brooker." Obituary, *Montreal Star*, 16 April 1955.

Design: Eiko Emori
Printing: Shannon Image Graphics